The Weather

Pandemic Poetry

Editor: Martin Rieser

Bristol Stanza Poets

Liz Cashdan
Richard Devereux
Richard Doyle
Kate Firth
Emily Fox
Lisa Lopresti
Agata Palmer
Marie Papier
David Punter
Martin Rieser
Jim Sidgwick
Pauline Sewards
Dave Wynne Jones
Peter Weinstock

Tangent Books 2020
ISBN 9781914345005

Cover Artwork and Design by Martin Rieser

Present

Don't look over your shoulder
the world you knew has gone.

Look forward, if you must,
that future's not yet born,

which leaves the now, uncomfortable
now, where the signals break

and morning has passed too soon.
Now, where the figures rise like smoke

and mirrors crowd with ghosts
from east to west, from floor to ceiling.

Now, where we live without meaning.
Now, untie a ribbon of hope.

Plague

Coronavirus, March 2020 and the Book of Exodus, chaps. 8,9,10
For Claude

I remember the chirping song
of grasshoppers in wild-flowered fields
through high summer,

the croaking of frogs in the reeds,
clouds of gnats floating in mid-air,
hailstones rapping on our windows.

I remember how flies shared our picnics;
the bluebottle Francis Jammes celebrated in his poem
Prière pour aller au Paradis avec les Anes

I recited in front of my professors
when leaving college and received
the prize for diction. But I do not remember

frogs in our bedrooms and palaces,
nor locusts devouring my grandfather's crops,
nor swarms of flies invading our houses.

But I remember the one:Musca Domestica,
which chose our kitchen to hibernate ,
my mother called *Constanza.*

Passover 2020

I know as the youngest I had to ask the question:
why is this night different from all other nights
but I never listened carefully to the answers.
Not sure I can remember all the plagues –
there are flies, there are boils, there is darkness.
The last plague is the death of the first-born, so
finally Pharoah will relent and let my people go.

With luck the Angel of the Lord who strikes the first born
will pass over the houses marked with blood.
Tonight I have made a notice with a red marker:
please leave the groceries in the box, then knock.
I've hung the sign on the door to the street
with a piece of string and there is a light
shining on it because it's a late-night slot.

I need to make sure that the Tesco delivery man
does not pass over my door. But by 10 pm
I have dozed off in front of the TV and I am startled
by the knocking. The groceries are in the box.
Does the delivery man know he is the Angel of the Lord.

Liz Cashdan

Resistance

you flew in on invisible wings
spirit-stealer, breath-taker
you circle in silence; you gather a storm

unseeable demon
you creep into my thinking
to infect me with dread: yet

here in my heart
I will meet and defeat you:
I am love

I have sky on my side, I have mist
I am mountain, oak-filled forest
I am moon and sun

I grow green shoots, ferns and conifer
I am sea and wave
I am love

deep in my weakness
I have found strength;
though you will batter me

tonight I shall bend
like the willow
you may not stick your suckered cells

upon my mind; my thoughts
will thwart you
I am too supple for your claws

I am clouds you cannot grasp
I am light- fighter
blackbird-dawn song

I am bud-burst springtime
sun-ray, hope-beam-rainbow
I am love

Kate Firth

Shock Tactics

Winter sunshine has enticed
our cold-water swimming brigade,
clad in tent-like thermal, hooded gowns.

Drawn to the sea-refreshed Clevedon pool,
we congregate and chat, whilst stripping off,
ready to brave the nine-and-a-half degrees.

Down the metal steps – you're not going to die!
Launch yourself; embrace the chill!
The shock of warm flesh into icy-cold

jolts the bejesus out of you.
After a minute or two,
numbness begins to soothe.

Buoyed up by the salt,
you can then stretch out
and loosely kick your feet.

But you must get out before
the freezing grip percolates your core.
Dripping, lobster pink, you're on fire:

invigorated beyond belief,
renewed, exchanging wide smiles
with fellow swimmers, born-again wild.

Jim Sidgwick

Lockdown Haiku

walk down an empty
street, gulls cackle, clear blue sky
zombie time is here

after the rain, masked
faces, strange pavement dances
fitful ghosts emerge

Richard Doyle

Pulse

Her panting gives steady rhythm
to our quiet, empty days.
Too empty, so I teach yoga and
give, give,
give, give,
give, give,
over Zoom – of course – a hundred
sessions in the first sixty days.
It props me with purpose, you see.
She snores through each meditation.

The beat of her tail hitting the floor,
is the response to sweet nothings I say,
a metronome of our simple joy
the pulse that is keeping me sane.

She's wagging, I'm missing my people,
we are barking lonely together.

Daily figures quote a sharp rise –
for many their vital pulse will stop.

The throb of her paws on the wooden floor
is the drumroll for our walk, the passport
to the outdoors, the daily alibi
for me and the dog,
my shrink extraordinaire,
my only certainty.

Agata Palmer

Mr Greenwood

First glimpsed -
a blur of green
beating a hasty retreat
over the garden fence
after feasting on fallen sunflower seeds.

Less elusive or undercover -
the sound of his yodelling call:
a distinctive *yaffle*, announcing his presence,
occasionally heard echoing
through neighbourhood gardens and trees.

Seldom seen close up,
until that morning, when,
pursued by the clatter of magpies
and an excited flurry of blue-tits,
he swooped into the apple tree,

lodging himself onto an upright bough,
as if he was taking up permanent residence,
merging with the autumn colours,
statue-still,
crampon claws gripping tight.

The green woodpecker then dropped down
onto the patch of well-raked grass
to forage for grubs and ants –
prodigious dagger-beak
lancing, probing, pitch-forking.

In between these dextrous brandishings,
he's head-up, vigilant, alert.
Robin Hood green, with scarlet
skull-cap streak; pale ringed eye
set in mask-like black.

Once a harbinger of rain,
it was posture and markings
which gave him the presence
to strut his stuff
and command centre stage.

The day of the funeral in lockdown

The cat stretched out a leg,
then another,
moving quite slowly

The rain
on the glass roof
beating, like small fists

like tears
running down
the cheeks of the world

I imagine
people who know you,
moving quite slowly

waking to the realisation
that it is the day of the funeral
in Lockdown

Not much to do today
but listen to the rain
on the glass roof

The sky, sad and grey,
staying close to the ground
for comfort

Femme Fatale

Is this evil scourging the world
male or female?
wonders the French Academy who,
thinking Coronavirus is as much an enemy
to the nation as Anglicism or other pests, opted –
in spite of the name ending in a consonant –
for the feminine.

The world's ears pricked up:
How can anyone deliberate on
the gender of a monster when life or
death are at stake?

The French do, calling *covid, 'la'*.
The Establishment prevailed, Covid
would be feminine. Another slap
to the French Feminists whose
choleric temper wouldn't hesitate to
blow up the Institution.

Thank God the English don't bother
about the sex of …
anything.

The Great Cunctator

I often dream in anachronism
when someone who could not have been
present, suddenly appears, transported
across the years. Last night, I was sixteen.

The Prime Minister wasn't Harold,
but Boris. I pulled on the balaclava
I bought last year, took an aerosol
and went through all the palaver

of blankets & rope ladders,
scaled the wall of my daughter's school,
ten foot high with razor-wire,
and dropped down, eager fool,

on a freezing night, fifty years ago,
into the yard at Stourbridge Grammar
(a hundred yards above the cut,
my industrial landscape Classics-crammer)

where I sprayed on the milk-shed wall
BORIS IS A CUNCTATOR
which, as he might know,
refers to the Roman Dictator

Quintus Fabius Maximus Verrucosus,
'The Delayer'.

Richard Devereux

The Unknown Carer

By bedsides, in kitchens, at home. Alone,
in line, behind masks in shops . Unpaid.

The washing machine for company: the rumbling, the mumbling,
the pain, and the broken connections

groans, ill-judged comments, unfiltered blurtings,
accusations; and pain

Social life: the counter staff at the chemist, the district nurse,
and the answerphone

of the DWP They've got it wrong again, can that be an accident,
or is dementia there too?

The hurt, the anger, the abandonment; crying in the night,
frustration, it shouldn't be like this.

Then the cold night-bus, back to an empty house
where voices once made memories.

Suggestion: create 'The Day of The Universal Carer' perhaps on
All Angels Day: 29th September. To commemorate it, place a wreath
or a rainbow of flowers at the plinth of the Unknown Carer
(Rename: Colston's Plinth in Bristol)

Pete Weinstock

Making a Day of It

A snatch of Harry Belafonte on the radio
singing ‘Mary’s Boy Child’, though it isn’t Christmas.

A small girl in the park picking up a hazel twig
stopping, ambushed in a green hush, as she whips it.

Two robins on the lawn prancing preening in dignity
outside my bee-bombarded study window.

My grand-daughter feeding swans by the lake
while they produce a glare she will later perceive as malevolent.

High fading contrails producing, for a poised moment,
a perfect letter X; immediately erased.

A solicitor’s sign advertising ‘Wills, bequests, debt advice’;
furtive movement behind the smoked panes.

Somewhere else the unheard roar of oceans,
the slow smashing of tectonic plates; lava-flow.

What is it, this gift of sewing fragments together
to make a multicoloured, imperfect day?

Seven Pomegranate Seeds

When she arrives, she is daybreak;
sunrise, on a dew spun meadow at dawn.
Clean and alert, she is a foal's first steps
on shaky feet, eager, and green
so keen to run before she can walk.

When she settles, she is noon in July;
burning, too bright for more than glances.
Tempered and controlled, she is a lioness's crouch
on silent paws, soft, and deadly:
she does not leap until she is ready.

When she knows she must return, she is sunset;
dissipating warmth, head tilted to the sky.
Coiled and skittish, she is a captive snake
spring loaded, sharp, and quick
she cannot slither from her fate.

When she leaves, I am a starless midnight;
white moon, chasing the sun across the sky.
Vast and empty, I am a black bear's slumber
in silent caverns, unarmed and vulnerable,
ready to crawl back into the sun.

Emily Fox

Messages

We created on the patio,

messages and pictures to God

with chalk.

What we wanted to convey

was legion

certain, he could see them

from space.

Now I would be one of

the raindrops

that hurtles explosively

down

to obliterate them

into colourful frothiness.

Things I don’t do anymore

I’m quite happy to leave cleaning the tops of cupboards
and if I don’t mow the lawn, it’ll last till spring.
I don’t need to hoover under the bed – it’s out of sight.
And this summer I didn’t wash the sitting room curtains.
I haven’t scrubbed the burnt grease off the oven sides
since I moved in so it’s not even my grease.
And so what if I don’t take the books down
off the shelves to dust one by one.
There’s no one to notice.

But if I give up on learning Russian,
if I stop struggling with Cyrillic script, and words
I can’t get my tongue around , who will there be
on winter mornings as I look out into the frozen garden,
who will there be to echo my mother’s voice reciting
Pushkin’s poem: *Maroz y solntse: dyen chudestny*.
Frost and sunshine: a splendid day.

Liz Cashdan

Weltanschauung in Pandemic

Sometime after riding the morphine train
between humiliation and trauma
you find your true purpose.
After you have left your body,
clean organs placed on ice,
your carapace becomes a gift to earth
of no more or less importance than worms
beetles, microcopia who feast on liquifying flesh.

You form a mineral nourishment
for trees planted in groups of three,
holding hands like school children,
supporting each other for a common good.
Roots will grow into you and you will grow into roots.
Branches and leaves reaching to sky.
Were you ever anything more
than a twinkle of hope?

The virus knows nothing of its host.
It is an actor, its only script to become more of itself.

Pauline Sewards

Waiting for Cherries

He chooses them wisely
picks only those twinned
at the stem: with tender
touch, he lays every
pair side by side
in a brown paper bag

At home, he places
his choice in a dish, waits
with pride as the dyads
of hard shiny bullets
ripen to plump purple spheres.
Then he watches her pick

up each pair
from the bowl, pull
stem from stem;
pluck off the stalk; he looks
at her lips she bites
through the skin

eyeing her mouth
to witness her taste
sweet juice
on her tongue.
Stares as she spits
out the stone

sighs as she sighs

Kate Firth

The Thebans

What with this and that, the Gods were most displeased
And agreed: the Thebans must be taught a lesson.
But what? And how? Poseidon volunteered
To raise a mighty wave and wash them clean
Away. But Athena pointed out that Thebes
Lies many miles inland, beyond his reach,
And a wave would wash away both good and bad.
Almighty Zeus said he had thunderbolts
Primed and ready to fire. The others demurred:
What Thebes deserves is a short, sharp shock but not
Annihilation of the most emphatic sort.
From Demeter, the bountiful, a thought:
To let the harvest fail until they have
Their fill of going short should give them time
To reflect, repent and renounce their feckless ways.
The realists said there was no point: they never
Would. And so, a lesson, yes, but what?

Apollo had been silent all this while.resistance
'My remit in our Councils is to keep
All safe, who should be safe, and free of dread
Disease. Yet, in the quiver on my back
I keep an arrow tipped with deadly juices from a bat.
Once, when circumstance required, I fired a shot
That caused a pestilence and plague to rage
Throughout a land; they died before they learned,
But when learned, they did not die.
The ones who lived were those who stopped to think
Where they went wrong. Their fear was great. They stayed
Indoors not going out least they should fall
Ill next – when hope was slim. Better men emerged.

For Thebes, he claimed, contagion fits the bill.
They all agreed: Apollo raised his bow
And laid low the Kingdom of Oedipus.

Richard Devereux

Film pitch

So this is my film of *The Secret Agent**

A London street.

Any street.

Political upsets. Terrorist alerts.

A police detective on the trail of known criminal suspects.

Verloc and the Professor.

An unassuming shopfrront.

Desperation.

Gritty men, anarchists,

half-crazy, uncertain,

women without power,

a confused boy growing up in a hot political climate.

Clambering to the top of truth.

** The Secret Agent, Joseph Conrad (1907)*

We are who we are…

intricate and light as a bee's wing

she bumbles through life in dappled sunlight

harvest mouse smiles for the change of seasons

dampened by the life that aisles us into categories

but she hovers above this abyss

without ever looking at who is looking back

hydrangea blue depends on where you are rooted

as all that is natural   exists

Two fireworks

Pushed through a letterbox they destroy
two houses, two dogs, and a cat.

Light a candle for lost lives and wonder
who watched and who fled the conflagration.

Charred houses, made of non-standard materials
are wall-eyed now. All that remains

is a molten motorbike in the front yard,
gleaming like a pair of muscular arms.

November 5th is over but all weekend the night
bears a freight of explosions and animal cries.

Whole streets reach for the Xanax.
Depends where you're looking from, and the double glazing,

whether the sky is radiant with cascading jewels
or clustered with spits of spite.

Statues

At the daily briefing, some minister or other
steps up to the dais, flanked or not
by career scientists, all public figures,
or figureheads, their status reinforced
by a background of wood panelling,
union jacks, campaign slogans to the fore,
spinning statistics on wide-screen slides.
Performances are stage-managed, questions
pre-selected, cut off if too searching.
They hold the whip hand,
tell us what to do, what to think.
We look up to them, like statues, placed
on pedestals amidst our civic life.

Respect, embedded in the very language,
conditions our measure of civility,
exercising power, not only fiscal,
that colonises the public space.
Are these graven images, cast bronzes
a form of idolatry, celebrating values,
beliefs, belonging to another era?
Dissent or protest, sinks under their weight
embodying establishment inertia,
year after year, and buttressed by
the likes of Saville whose charity work

hid his paedophilia in plain sight,
or Colston, attempting to expiate, perhaps,
the sins of slavery, endowing schools, churches,
with not a single word of repentance.

Until another, unarmed, black man
is killed by a cop, provoking outrage,
anger, and then, in the comfort of the crowd,
people discover that they too have lost
too much, too often, for too long,
when that knowledge finally finds focus,
on a statue, long-resented, now pulled down,
rolled to the waterfront, dumped in the dock.

Elsewhere, the talking heads condemn the action,
know only too well they have a lot to lose,
their utterance haunted by an empty plinth.

Body, Female

When they find me
in the first rain below
September skies,
I am six weeks gone and
Three
Feet
Underground.

Barely covered (with moss and dirt,
in the news,
by the lace he left me in).

The rain forges new rivers
Along the crevice of my clavicle.

My dying breath caught (on the wind,
in your palm,
between my teeth).

The hollow of my ribcage now
a new cavern for the stream to pool.

My body split (like your half-moon smile,
by county lines,
between here and nowhere).

Lost too early,
Fond too late.

Corvids

The crows have much to discuss
this day in November, craiking through
the beechwood with their lively chatter.

The birds must know a thing or two
about the state of play: knife-edge election, USA;
lockdown Europe and its losses.

A world turning away to winter,
leaves reeling down- drunk paratroopers,
light golden through unshed clusters.

We sit in sunshine, calm in the breeze
and talk gently of the years passed and passing,
late autumn furled in leaf litter, listening for the sirens.

Scipio Africanus.

They have vandalised a gravestone in my parish;
perhaps the only black grave in the churchyard.
Certainly, the only one that could be identified as such
amongst the fading names on headstones,
polished marble of family tombs, war graves,
but you'd have to seek it out.
Chubby black cherubs give the game away
and may be in bad taste like the inscription,
a kind of spiritual colonialism, celebrating salvation,
but let's not forget, all faiths are evangelical,
fishers of men, women, and in this case
a pagan child imported to die
at just eighteen, three hundred years ago.

His name, Scipio Africanus, teases with uncertainties.
Was it his master's intention he should be freed
for good service, the practice of the Romans,
or only to celebrate another triumph
over the African power that was Carthage?
We cannot know; the master did not long
outlive the man. What is certain is
black Christians too have been evangelists,
empowering Gospel, Soul music, speaking in tongues,
or George Floyd on a sport discipleship
to save youth from the gun.

This city has a black mayor, evangelical
in faith and politics, "the Reverend Rees,"
who receives death threats from the self-same gang
that vandalises historic gravestones;
the dispossessed, disenfranchised, disempowered,
becoming more unstable under lockdown,
living as people are not meant to live,
in fear; the very people that Rees fights for,
now energised by a different agenda.

This is a broad church; hard by its north wall,
the Victorian grave of an Egyptologist;
her lesbian lover and daughter, is
marked by no cross; an obelisk and ankh,
bear witness to some ecumenical tolerance
of pagan Egypt, despite Israel's enslavement.

Let slip the rabid dogs and no golden calf,
enthroned in the heart of government,
can whistle them in to seek a Promised Land
where black lives matter.

Pale Rider

The hill is rain-dimmed;
shapes dance and glimmer.

'There's someone there, daddy, look -
up on that ledge'.

'No no, my lad, that's just
an old windswept thornbush'.

With manacles on his hands
waving at us, but his sight
is not to be borne.

'Daddy, daddy, he's moving towards us -
how can he come down the hill so fast?'

'No, my dear, it's only a couple of rocks
dislodged by the rain'.

How does he move with such mad urgency?
what does he need? Are those spurs
in place of feet?

'Daddy, he has a horse -
he's getting up on it!'

'There is no horse, dear heart,
only a mirage of the storm'.

Yet I can see the dead nag's head
nodding and hear its breathlike a warning of pain.

'Daddy, I'm frightened -
how he comes so close!'

'Come on, it's just a rabbit
snuffling in the undergrowth'.

Then what are these silver droplets
cascading through the sky
turning the air white?

'Daddy, daddy, where are you?
I can't see you any more'.

'My son, my son, take my hand,
I'll lead you away from harm'.

But what is this grip like ice,
and why the drumming of waiting hooves;
can I bargain with you, pale rider?
ask you to stay a while?

My Type

Across the scale of time, these rivers are short-lived,
yet so crucial to you and me, their flow essential.
Hidden from rain, defiant of gravity, they need
powerful pumping action to flow reliably.
We cannot sail them together,
but we breathe the same air to oxygenate them.
No trees reflect in their current, they don't tend to flood.
Their meanderings can be traced just under the skin.

These rivers run from me and into me, I am the source
and the destination, the spring and millions of tiny deltas,
as they release into the fertile fields of my cells,
fields empty of hedges and birdsong, but rich
in the essence of my being, at least for the duration.
Pretty good design, if not for the wear & tear
                                        of the whole system.
From wide to narrow runnels, they carry
intricacies science *thinks* we understand;
countless little pilgrims sent with messages
to every part of my territory. I hope it's good tidings.

I apply perfume where pulse is strong
so that the scent keeps giving.

Sometimes these canals get punctured for medical, accidental,
or self-destructing reasons – or haemorrhage in rebellion.
In some cases, they need re-filling with a suitable match –
I'm thankful to the donors of those three pints that have kept me here:
Whoever you were, immaterial – you're definitely my type.